Oregon

Rich Smith

Visit us at
www.abdopublishing.com

Published by ABDO Publishing Company, 8000 West 78th Street, Suite 310, Edina, Minnesota 55439 USA. Copyright ©2010 by Abdo Consulting Group, Inc. International copyrights reserved in all countries. No part of this book may be reproduced in any form without written permission from the publisher. The Checkerboard Library™ is a trademark and logo of ABDO Publishing Company.

Printed in the United States.

Editor: John Hamilton
Graphic Design: Sue Hamilton
Cover Illustration: Neil Klinepier
Cover Photo: iStock Photo
Interior Photo Credits: Alamy, AP Images, Canton Photo-Gresham, Corbis, Dan & Linda Dzurisin-Vancouver WA, Dennis Galloway/Hult Center for the Performing Arts, Enchanted Forest, Evergreen Aviation & Space Museum, Garland Landmark Society, Getty, Gracie Films/20th Century Fox TV, Granger Collection, Henk Rayer, Independence National Historical Park/Artist C.W. Peale, iStock Photo, Joni Huntley, Jupiterimages, Library of Congress, Mile High Maps, Mountain High Maps, National Library of Medicine, National Park Service, New Line Cinema, North Wind Picture Archives, One Mile Up, *The Oregonian*, Peter Arnold Inc, Rick Leche, Tom Brandt, and the U.S. Postal Service.
Statistics: State population statistics taken from 2008 U.S. Census Bureau estimates. City and town population statistics taken from July 1, 2007, U.S. Census Bureau estimates. Land and water area statistics taken from 2000 Census, U.S. Census Bureau.

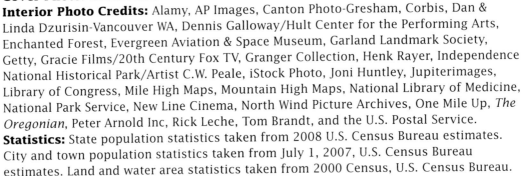

Manufactured with paper containing at least 10% post-consumer waste

Library of Congress Cataloging-in-Publication Data

Smith, Rich, 1954-
  Oregon / Rich Smith.
     p. cm. -- (The United States)
  Includes index.
  ISBN 978-1-60453-672-0
  1. Oregon--Juvenile literature. I. Title.

F876.3.S66 2010
979.5--dc22
                              2008052395

Table of Contents

The Beaver State 4

Quick Facts 6

Geography 8

Climate and Weather 12

Plants and Animals 14

History 18

Did You Know? 24

People 26

Cities 30

Transportation 34

Natural Resources 36

Industry 38

Sports 40

Entertainment 42

Timeline 44

Glossary 46

Index 48

The Beaver State

Oregon is located on the coast of the rainy but mild Pacific Northwest. Oregon offers natural wonders, fine cities, friendly people, good schools, and many fun things to do.

Oregon's nickname is the Beaver State. Early trappers caught many beavers in Oregon, which were prized for their pelts. Today, the state continues to attract important businesses. Nike, the world's biggest maker of athletic shoes, has its main office in Oregon. Ships sailing from the Port of Portland export huge amounts of wheat to other countries. And the state's largest private employer is Intel, the maker of microprocessor chips found in most personal computers.

Heceta Head Lighthouse overlooks Oregon's wild and beautiful coastline.

Quick Facts

STATE OF OREGON

1859

Name: Uncertain. Many believe Oregon comes from the word Ouragan, which was the local Native American name for the Columbia River.

State Capital: Salem, population 151,913

Date of Statehood: February 14, 1859 (33rd state)

Population: 3,790,060 (27th-most populous state)

Area (Total Land and Water): 98,381 square miles (254,806 sq km), 9th-largest state

Largest City: Portland, population 550,396

Nickname: The Beaver State

Motto: *Alis volat propriis* (She flies with her own wings)

State Bird: Western Meadowlark

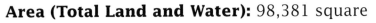

Oregon Grape

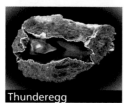

Thunderegg

Douglas Fir

State Flower: Oregon Grape

State Rock: Thunderegg

State Tree: Douglas Fir

State Song: "Oregon, My Oregon"

Highest Point: 11,239 feet (3,426 m), Mt. Hood

Lowest Point: 0 feet (0 m), Pacific Ocean

Average July Temperature: 60°F (16°C) (coastal); 72°F (22°C) (southeast)

Record High Temperature: 119°F (48°C) in Pendleton, August 10, 1898

Average January Temperature: 45°F (7°C) (coastal); 27°F (-3°C) (southeast)

Record Low Temperature: -54°F (-48°C) in Seneca, February 10, 1933

Average Annual Precipitation: 27 inches (69 cm)

Number of U.S. Senators: 2

Number of U.S. Representatives: 5

U.S. Postal Service Abbreviation: OR

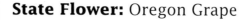

Mt. Hood

Geography

Oregon is the nation's ninth-largest state. It covers 98,381 square miles (254,806 sq km).

Oregon has eight natural regions. First is the Coastal region. Its sandy beaches and tree-covered rocky cliffs gradually give way to a range of low mountains with many small lakes.

East of the Coastal region is the pleasant Willamette Valley region. Most of the people in Oregon live there.

The Cascade Mountains region runs north to south through the middle of the state. The region includes Oregon's tallest peaks.

The mostly flat Columbia River Plateau region is east of the Cascades. Its rich farm soil was created by towering volcanoes that almost completely buried themselves beneath their own lava.

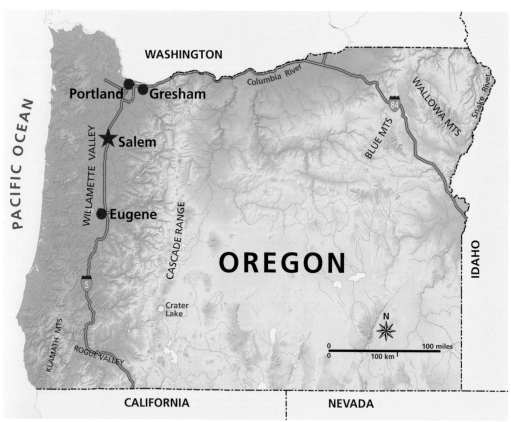

OREGON

Oregon's total land and water area is 98,381 square miles (254,806 sq km). It is the 9th-largest state. The state capital is Salem.

To the northeast are the forest-covered Blue and Wallowa Mountains. And along Oregon's border with Idaho is the region of the Snake River. Several high dams have been built there to make electricity.

The Southeastern Lake region is a desert. It is located south of the Columbia River Plateau.

In the southwest corner of the state is the Klamath Mountain region. A large part of that region is taken up by the fertile Rogue Valley.

Running along most of Oregon's northern border with Washington is the Columbia River. This is the state's most important river, and among the largest in North America. Oregon's other major rivers are the Willamette, Deschutes, John Day, and Rogue Rivers.

The John Day Dam is used to create electricity.

Crater Lake was formed when Mount Mazama erupted 7,700 years ago. The mountain collapsed, leaving a bowl-shaped caldera, or volcanic crater. Centuries of rain and snow filled the caldera, creating Crater Lake.

The most beautiful of the state's many lakes is Crater Lake. It sits in the cone of a 6,000-foot (1,829-m) -high extinct volcano. Crater Lake is one of North America's deepest lakes.

Climate and Weather

Oregon has two types of climate. In the west, temperatures are mild throughout the year because of cool, moist winds that blow inland from the Pacific Ocean. They keep the air from becoming too hot or cold.

Also, much rain falls in western Oregon. Some areas receive almost 200 inches (508 cm) of rain during a normal year.

Heavy rains cause a road to flood near Ashland, Oregon.

The high Cascade Mountains in the middle of Oregon stop most of the rain from reaching the state's eastern half. That causes large parts of the region to be a desert. The Cascade Mountains block not only the rain but also the Pacific Ocean winds. Without those winds, temperatures in eastern Oregon become very hot during the summer and bitterly cold during the winter.

The desert area of the Painted Hills at John Day Fossil Beds National Monument in eastern Oregon.

Plants and Animals

Oregon is famous for its wildflowers. Among the most beautiful are larkspur, iris, leafy aster, calypso orchid, and red columbine. The state wildflower is the stream violet or pioneer violet.

Stream Violet

Trees common in Oregon east of the Cascades include mahogany, ponderosa pine, and western juniper. In the drier parts of the state are found sagebrush and shrubs, such as green manzanita.

West of the Cascade Mountains, Oregon is home to some of the world's most lush rainforests. Evergreen trees include Douglas fir, white fir, pine, and giant redwood. There are also plenty of alder, maple, oak, ash, cedar, larch, mountain hemlock, alpine fir, and spruce.

The Sitka spruce is one of Oregon's largest trees. They can grow more than 200 feet (61 m) tall.

At 620 feet (189 m), Multnomah Falls is the tallest waterfall in Oregon. It is in a lush, green forest.

More than 480 kinds of birds can be found in Oregon. They include ducks, geese, loons, pelicans, cormorants, quails, pheasants, wild turkeys, sapsuckers, chickadees, finches, woodpeckers, hawks, eagles, and owls.

The largest animals found in Oregon are deer, elk, antelope, and bear. Smaller animals include foxes, bobcats, coyotes, skunks, rabbits, chipmunks, raccoons, badgers, minks, river otters, and beavers. Along the coast are found sea lions, seals, crabs, starfish, and turtles.

Some meat-eating animals that live along the rivers of western Oregon survive by catching salmon. Salmon are the state's most important fish. Other fish that

swim the rivers, lakes, and coastline of Oregon include trout, bass, perch, halibut, tuna, cod, and smelt.

A salmon in Oregon's Rogue River.

The beaver is Oregon's state mammal.

Spotted Owl

Harbor Seal

Starfish, Sea Anemones & Urchins

History

Many Native Americans lived in Oregon before the coming of European explorers. One of the larger tribes was the Chinook. They lived in villages along the

Native Americans used nets to catch salmon in the Columbia River.

Columbia River and enjoyed catching salmon.

The first European to see Oregon was Spain's Bartolome Ferrelo in 1543. He sailed along the coast. Sir Francis Drake of England explored Oregon's coast in 1579. He was searching for the Northwest Passage. This was a water route he believed might exist between the Pacific and Atlantic Oceans.

In 1805, American explorers Meriwether Lewis and William Clark traveled into Oregon by land from the East. They also were looking for the Northwest Passage. Such a water route would make sending trade goods from coast to coast much easier. Unfortunately, the Northwest Passage never existed. But Lewis and Clark did discover the wonder and beauty of Oregon.

Meriwether Lewis and William Clark ended their westward trek across America when they hit the Pacific Ocean. The expedition built Fort Clatsop near today's Astoria, Oregon, spending the winter of 1805-1806 in the fort. A replica of Fort Clatsop stands in Oregon today.

In 1811, Astoria became the first permanent settlement in Oregon. It was founded by John Jacob Astor's Pacific Fur Company.

In the early 1800s, hundreds of fur trappers came to Oregon. In 1811, some of those trappers built a trading post at the mouth of the Columbia River. They named it Astoria, which later became a city.

The population of Oregon really began to grow in the early 1840s with the arrival of pioneers. They came to Oregon in covered wagons. These brave travelers started in Missouri and followed a path known as the Oregon Trail.

The Oregon Trail was too difficult and dangerous for the most common covered wagon of that day. So, a special covered wagon called a prairie schooner was built and used instead.

A prairie schooner was smaller and lighter than a regular covered wagon.

In 1848, Oregon became a territory of the United States. It was granted statehood on Valentine's Day, February 14, 1859. When the Civil War started in 1861, Oregon did not join the rebel South. It remained in the Union. The Civil War finally ended in 1865.

The people of Portland, Oregon, celebrate statehood.

In the years after the Civil War, more and more people everywhere needed wood. Oregon's timber industry grew. Railroads

A year's worth of logs are ready to float down the Columbia River in 1902.

were built across the state to help move logs from the forests to the sawmills, and then to waiting ships at ports along major rivers and the coast.

Bonneville Dam

The timber industry helped Oregon's economy increase during the 1880s and 1890s. More people came to the state. More kinds of businesses started, and cities arose. In the middle of the 1900s, Oregon built mighty dams on some of its rivers to make electricity. The electricity made it possible for Oregon's cities and ports to modernize.

In the 1960s, Oregon citizens worried that their modern ways were hurting the environment. That led the state to pass laws telling people and businesses they had to be kinder to nature. Today, Oregon is one of the most Earth-friendly states in America.

Did You Know?

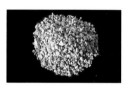

- Zeolite is a mineral found in Oregon. It is used to keep aquarium water fresh.

- *The Simpsons* TV series takes place in Springfield. But viewers are never told which state Springfield is in. At least 35 states have a city with all or part of the name being Springfield. Could it be Oregon? *The Simpsons* creator Matt Groening is from Oregon.

- Oregon is the only state whose flag has different images on each side. On one side is the state seal and on the other is the state animal, the beaver.

- Hollywood movies are sometimes shot in Oregon. Examples include *Kindergarten Cop*, *Teenage Mutant Ninja Turtles 3*, *Short Circuit*, *Homeward Bound*, and *Free Willy*.

- In a single year, freight trains on Oregon's Portland and Western Railroad haul more than 90,000 carloads of wood chips, paper, and harvested crops.

- Gold mining once was important work in Oregon. Now it is just a fun hobby. Gold hunters today search for tiny bits of gold in Oregon's many streams and creeks.

People

Matt Groening (1954-) is a famous cartoonist, screenwriter, and producer. He first wrote and drew a newspaper cartoon. Its popularity led to him to create a television cartoon, *The Simpsons*. Later, he created a science-fiction cartoon, *Futurama*. Groening has won many honors, including several Emmy Awards. Groening was born in Portland.

James Beard (1903–1985) was a famous chef and writer. He was born in Portland, and became known as the father of gourmet eating in America. Today, the James Beard Foundation gives money to help people who want to become professional cooks.

Bill Bowerman (1911–1999) was a University of Oregon track coach. He produced 31 Olympic athletes, 51 All-Americans, and 24 college athletics champions. He also was the co-founder of Nike. Trying to find a running shoe that weighed less, but had better grip and cushioning, he used his wife's waffle iron to create the first waffle-sole shoe. This helped make Nike one of the largest sports companies in the world. Bowerman was born in Portland.

Joni Huntley (1956–) is a teacher who earlier was a famous track star. In 1974, she set the American record in women's high jump. She then won the bronze medal in women's high jump during the 1984 Summer Olympics in Los Angeles. Huntley was born in McMinnville.

Mark Hatfield (1922–) was governor of Oregon from 1959 to 1967. He brought new types of industries to the state and asked that more money be spent on improved transportation systems. He served as a U.S. senator from Oregon from 1967 to 1997. He has written several books on war, politics, and politicians. Hatfield was born in Dallas, Oregon.

Thomas Lawson McCall (1913–1983) was Oregon's governor from 1967 to 1975. Many of the state's ideas about recycling and land are credited to McCall. He is remembered as the state's first strong protector of the environment.

Linus Carl Pauling (1901–1994) won the 1954 Nobel Prize in chemistry for helping scientists better understand molecules and chemical bonds. He won a second Nobel Prize in 1962 for working to bring peace to the world. Pauling was born in Portland, Oregon.

Cities

The largest city in Oregon is **Portland**. It has a population of about 550,396. The climate of Portland is perfect for growing roses. There even is an annual festival and parade to celebrate the rose.

That is why Portland's nickname is The City of Roses. Portland also is famous for its many fine bakeries, and for its system of buses and trains that help people get from place to place.

The capital of Oregon is **Salem**. It has a population of about 151,913. The city has many government buildings. It also has many cherry trees. In fact, Salem's nickname is Cherry City. Salem is a major food processing center.

The city of **Eugene** is about as big as Salem. It has a population of 149,004. Eugene is famous for its love of theater and sports. Because of that, Eugene officially calls itself "The World's Greatest City of the Arts and Outdoors."

The Hult Center for the Performing Arts is in downtown Eugene. It has a beautiful theater, art gallery, and museum.

Just to the east of Portland is the city of **Gresham**. It is the fourth-largest city in Oregon. Gresham is one of the state's fastest growing cities. People like living in Gresham because of its beauty and charm. It has a population of 99,721.

The city of Gresham
is known for its beauty and charm.
It is one of Oregon's fastest growing cities.

Transportation

Oregon's system of transportation is among the best in the world. Ocean-going cargo ships come and go from ports in Portland on the Columbia and Willamette Rivers, and from a port in Coos Bay on the southwest Oregon coast.

A large cargo ship is loaded with wheat at the Port of Portland.

Oregon is served by at least 30 important railroad companies. Among the largest are the Union Pacific Railroad and Amtrak.

Portland's Union Station is the city's center of passenger train transportation.

The biggest of the nearly 100 public airports in Oregon is Portland International Airport. The Oregon National Guard has a jet fighter base in one corner of Portland International Airport.

Interstate 5 is the main north-south highway. It runs from the state of Washington into California. The other main highway is Interstate 84, which runs west to east. It begins at Interstate 5 in Portland and stretches past the border of Idaho.

Natural Resources

Farms and ranches in Oregon earn more than $4 billion each year. They make the most money by growing flowers. Cattle ranching and dairy farming are also important. Hay, ryegrass, and wheat are among the state's major crops.

Along with their crops, many Oregon farmers are putting wind turbines on their land to generate electricity.

Mined minerals for which Oregon is famous include construction sand, gravel, and crushed stone. The state ranks at or near the top for its output of pumice, perlite, talc, diatomite, and various types of zeolite.

Thanks to its many forests, Oregon leads the nation in the production of softwood lumber. Even so, the state's timber industry is shrinking because of rules protecting the environment.

Pine trees are harvested from some of Oregon's many forests.

Oregon's fishing industry reels in big catches of salmon, tuna, Pacific whiting, halibut, crab, and many others.

Industry

Businesses prefer to be located in places that their workers enjoy. Businesses also like being where it is easy to bring in raw materials and ship out finished products. Oregon is just such a place.

One of Oregon's most important industries is high-technology. The state has a number of leading companies that create, sell, repair, or improve computer products. Many of these companies are bunched together in a section of the Willamette Valley that people call the Silicon Forest.

Major companies in other types of industries also find Oregon a welcoming place. The city of Beaverton is where sporting-goods giant Nike has its headquarters.

Nike's beautiful world headquarters is located near Beaverton, Oregon.

Medford is home to a pair of superstars in the field of mail-order retailing. Harry and David sells fruits and gifts, and Musician's Friend sells music and instruments. In Portland there are book publishing businesses, insurance companies, banks, and import-export firms.

Sports

Oregon citizens are proud of their major league sports team, basketball's Portland Trail Blazers. The team formed in 1970.

Blaze, the mascot of the Portland Trail Blazers, dunks a ball at the Rose Garden Arena in Portland, Oregon.

In 1977, the Trail Blazers won their first national championship. Several players have gone on to be named to the Basketball Hall of Fame.

Portland also has teams that play minor-league baseball. Salem and Eugene each have one minor-league baseball team of their own.

College sports are popular in Oregon. Football games played by teams from Oregon State University and the University of Oregon often play very exciting contests.

Oregon is a fisherman's paradise. Boating, hiking, wakeboarding, and wind surfing are favorite outdoor pastimes. So are kayaking and river rafting. Many Oregon people enjoy bicycle riding.

People enjoy many different types of sports in Oregon.

Entertainment

Love of paintings draws many visitors to the Portland Art Museum. But it is the love of dinosaurs that attracts others to the John Day Fossil Beds National Monument in eastern Oregon. There is a public area where anyone can dig for fossils.

In total, the state has more than 100 museums, historic sites, botanical gardens, and arboretums.

Fossils of a bison-sized mammal called an entelodon have been found in the area of the John Day Fossil Beds National Monument.

Best known are Portland's Oregon Museum of Science and Industry, Washington Park Zoo, Western Forestry Center, and the Oregon Historical Society's museum.

The Evergreen Aviation & Space Museum in McMinnville is home to the *Spruce Goose*. Built by aviator Howard Hughes, this

Evergreen Aviation & Space Museum

famous wooden aircraft only flew once, in November 1947.

In Ashland, an annual festival is held to celebrate the plays of William Shakespeare. Portland, Salem, and Eugene each have symphony orchestras. Portland also has a ballet troupe.

The Enchanted Forest is in Salem.

There are several major theme parks in Oregon. Among the best is Salem's Enchanted Forest. It is home to the Ice Mountain bobsled roller coaster.

Timeline

1543—Bartolome Ferrelo of Spain sails along Oregon's coast.

1579—English explorer Francis Drake explores Oregon's coast.

1805—Lewis and Clark reach Oregon by foot from the east. Their journey ends at the Pacific Ocean.

1811—First white settlement in Oregon is founded at Astoria.

1843—First wave of pioneers arrives after traveling by covered wagon along the Oregon Trail.

1859—Oregon becomes the 33rd state in the Union.

1884—Travel between Oregon and the rest of the United States by train becomes possible.

1938—Oregon builds its first hydroelectric dam. The Modern Era arrives.

1960s—Oregon becomes a pioneer in the environmental movement.

2002—A lightning strike sets off the Sour Biscuit Fire, scorching more than half a million acres (202,343 ha) in southern Oregon and northern California.

Glossary

Chinook—A Native American tribe that lived along the coast of the Pacific Ocean and along the banks of the Columbia River, including near present-day Oregon. The Chinook were known for their skills in building canoes and fishing.

Export—To send something from one country to another, usually for selling.

Fur Trapper—A person who catches animals for their soft, thick coats of hair, which is later made into warm clothing.

Gourmet—A person who likes very good-tasting food.

Import—To bring something into a country from another, usually for selling.

Kayak—An enclosed canoe with a small opening in the center of the top. A pole with paddles at each end is used to move the kayak through the water.

Molecules—One or more atoms joined together in a group. An atom is a tiny particle that is like a building block. In water, for example, two hydrogen atoms combine with an oxygen atom (H^2O) to create one water molecule.

Prairie Schooner—A small covered wagon made for travel over rocky, sandy, or mountainous trails.

Sawmill—A place that cuts logs into lumber.

Spruce Goose—A huge "flying boat" created by aviator Howard Hughes during World War II. Also called the Hughes H-4 *Hercules*, it was hoped that the big plane could transport war materials. Because there was so little metal available during wartime, the ship was built out of wood, although mostly birch (not spruce, as the nickname implies). Weighing 300,000 pounds (136,078 kg), and with a wingspan of 320 feet (98 m), it became one of the biggest airplanes ever built. Hughes flew the too-heavy plane only once, on November 2, 1947. Today, the plane is in the Evergreen Aviation & Space Museum in McMinnville, Oregon.

Index

A

America (*See* United States)
Amtrak 35
Ashland, OR 43
Astoria, OR 20
Atlantic Ocean 18

B

Basketball Hall of Fame 40
Beard, James 26
Beaverton, OR 38
Blue Mountains 10
Bowerman, Bill 27

C

California 4, 35
Cascade Mountain region 8
Cascade Mountains 8, 13, 14, 15
Chinook (tribe) 18
Civil War 21, 22
Clark, William 19
Coastal region 8
Columbia River 10, 18, 20, 34
Columbia River Plateau 10
Columbia River Plateau region 8
Coos Bay, OR 34
Crater Lake 11

D

Dallas, OR 28
Deschutes River 10
Drake, Francis 18

E

Earth 23
Emmy Award 26

Enchanted Forest 43
England 18
Eugene, OR 32, 40, 43
Evergreen Aviation & Space Museum 43

F

Ferrelo, Bartolome 18
Free Willy 25
Futurama 26

G

Gresham, OR 33
Groening, Matt 24, 26

H

Harry and David 39
Hatfield, Mark 28
Hollywood, CA 25
Homeward Bound 25
Hughes, Howard 43
Huntley, Joni 27

I

Ice Mountain bobsled roller coaster 43
Idaho 4, 10, 35
Intel 4

J

James Beard Foundation 26
John Day Fossil Beds National Monument 42
John Day River 10

K

Kindergarten Cop 25
Klamath Mountain region 10

L

Lewis, Meriwether 19
Los Angeles, CA 27

M

McCall, Thomas Lawson 28
McMinnville, OR 27, 43
Medford, OR 39
Missouri 20
Musician's Friend 39

N

National Guard 35
Nevada 4
Nike 4, 27, 38
Nobel Prize 29
North America 10, 11
Northwest Passage 18, 19

O

Olympics 27
Oregon Historical Society 43
Oregon Museum of Science and Industry 43
Oregon State University 41
Oregon Trail 20, 21

P

Pacific Northwest 4
Pacific Ocean 12, 13, 18
Pauling, Linus Carl 29
Port of Portland 4
Portland, OR 26, 27, 29, 30, 33, 34, 35, 39, 40, 43
Portland and Western Railroad 25
Portland Art Museum 42
Portland International Airport 35
Portland Trail Blazers 40

R

Rogue River 10
Rogue Valley 10

S

Salem, OR 31, 40, 43
Shakespeare, William 43
Short Circuit 25
Silicon Forest 38
Simpsons, The 24, 26
Snake River region 10
South 21
Southeastern Lake region 10
Spain 18
Springfield 24
Spruce Goose 43

T

Teenage Mutant Ninja Turtles 3 25

U

Union 21
Union Pacific Railroad 35
United States 21, 23, 26, 28
University of Oregon 27, 41

W

Wallowa Mountains 10
Washington 4, 10, 35
Washington Park Zoo 43
Western Forestry Center 43
Willamette River 10, 34
Willamette Valley 38
Willamette Valley region 8